MARCO RUBIO is RUNNING for PRESIDENT!

A 2016 Presidential Election Coloring Book

ISBN 978-1523408245
Cover design by Smerdloff
copyright 2016, all rights reserved.

I0442085

Marco Rubio is running for President.

He wants to live in the White House.

Marco Antonio
Rubio was born
in Miami, Florida,
on May 28, 1971.

He still lives in the Miami area, with his wife, Jeanette Dousbedes (his high school sweetheart, and a former Miami Dolphins cheerleader), and their four children.

Rubio is the son of Mario Rubio Reina and Oriales Rubio, who were born in Cuba and came to the United States in 1956, just ahead of Castro and the Communist takeover.

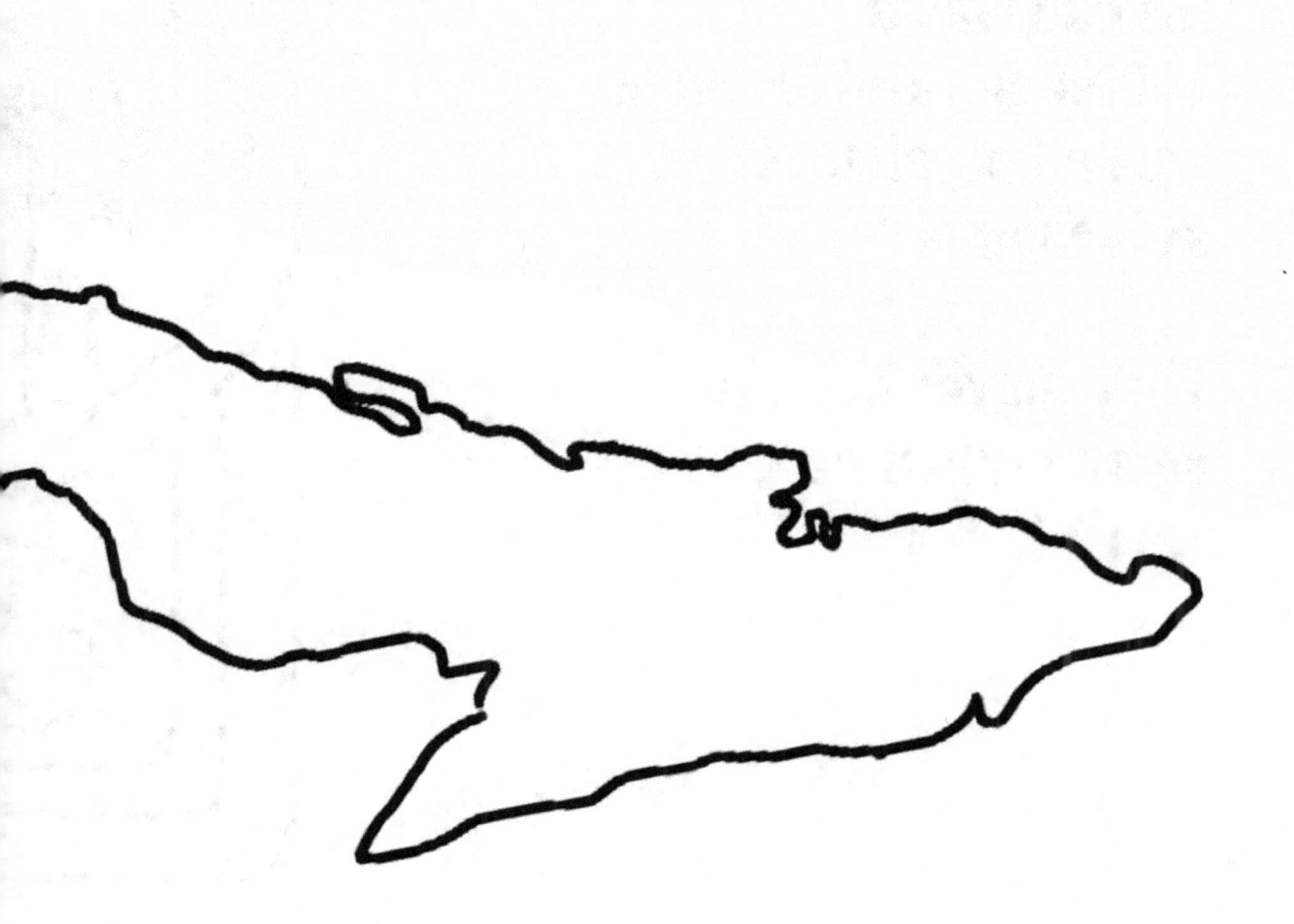

When he was 8,
Rubio's family moved
to Las Vegas.

His dad was a
bartender, and his mom
was a housekeeper
at a casino.

They moved back to
Miami when he
was 11.

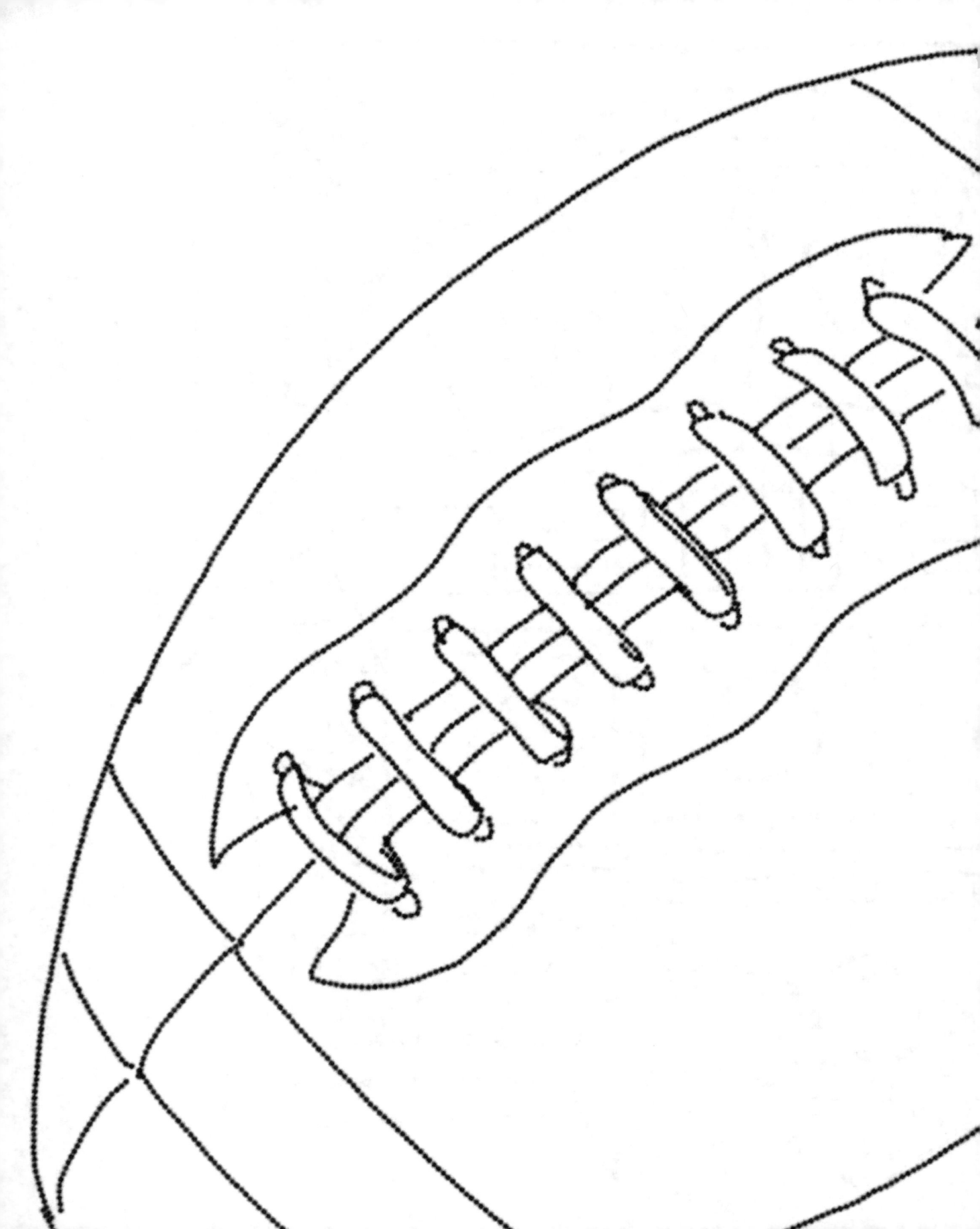

Rubio attended Tarkio College in Missouri. He was recruited to play football there.

After one year, he transferred to Santa Fe Community College, in Gainesville, Florida, and ultimately graduated from the University of Florida with a degree in political science, in 1993.

He attended law school at the University of Miami, and graduated in 1996.

In 1998, just two years out of law school, Marco Rubio was elected as City Commissioner in West Miami, Florida.

He was elected to the Florida House of Representatives in 2000, and reelected three times.

During these years, he worked as a lawyer with a Miami firm, and then as a lobbyist.

Rubio rose quickly through the House GOP leadership. In 2002 he became Majority Leader.
And in 2005, at the age of 34, he was chosen as the first Cuban-American Speaker of the Florida House of Representatives.

He served in that role until 2008.

He was elected to the U. S. Senate in 2010.

In 2013, Rubio was a member
of the "Gang of Eight"
U. S. Senators, who worked together
to craft a bipartisan immigration
reform bill. Their proposal created a
path to citizenship for undocumented
immigrants. as well as strengthening border
security in the future.

Rubio has said he would "repeal and replace" the Patient Protection and Affordable Care Act, proposing a tax credit to be used for health insurance, state-based high-risk pools where people could purchase insurance coverage, the expansion of Medical Savings Accounts, and changes to the funding of both Medicaid and Medicare.

Marco Rubio disputes the scientific evidence of global climate change, saying that human activity may not play a major role, and that proposals to address climate change would likely be ineffective and economically harmful.

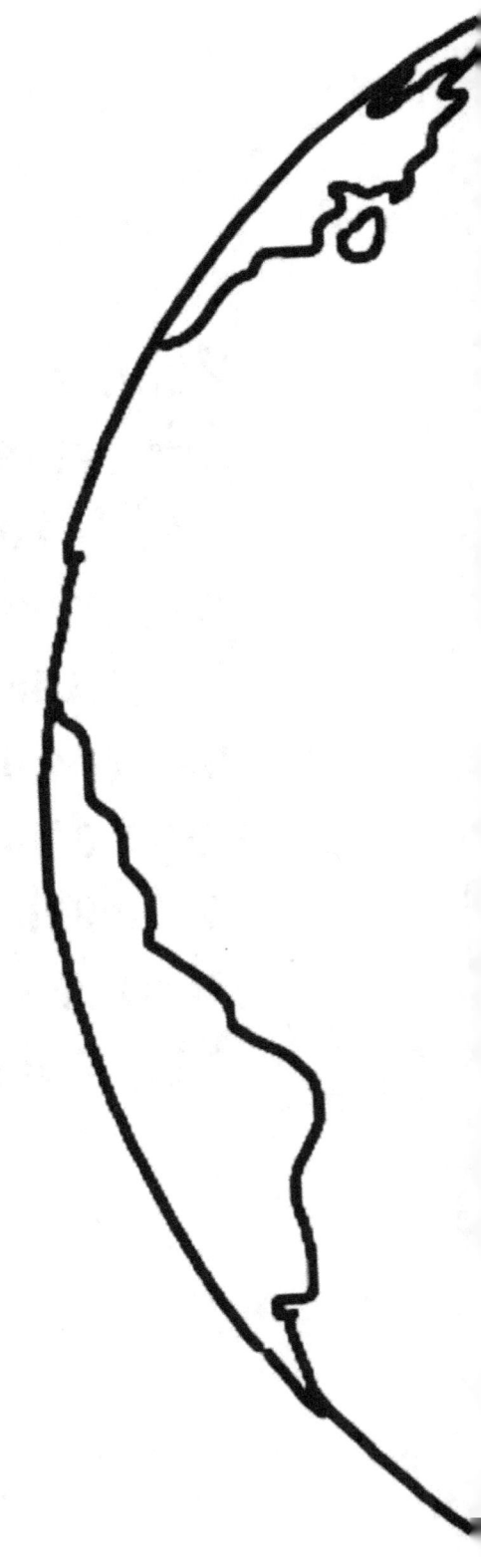

Rubio proposed the "Student Right to Know Before You Go Act," which would require colleges and universities to inform students--prior to taking out student loans--of the future income they might expect after obtaining a degree. The proposal would automatically base student loan payments on subsequent income as well, and students could partner with investors who could buy their loan debt in return for a percentage of future earnings.

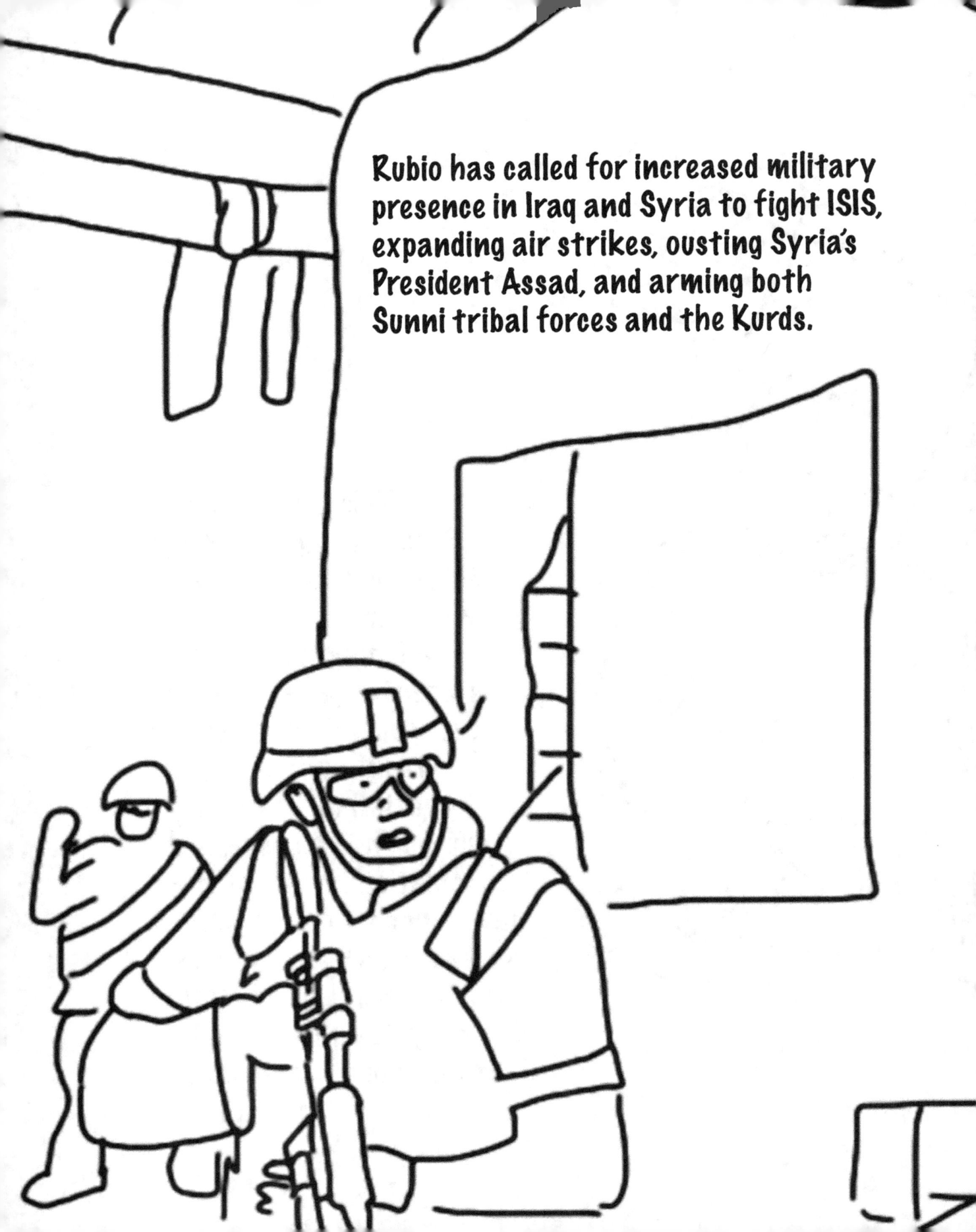

Marco Rubio has proposed a vastly simplified tax code, with just two rates: 15 percent up to $75,000 in income, and 35% for income above $75,000. He has called for reducing the corporate tax rate; eliminating capital gains taxes; and adding a new child tax credit for families.

Rubio says he would offset the estimated revenue
reduction (of several trillion dollars) through spending
cuts, including raising the Social Security eligibility age
and reducing Medicare spending.

November 8th, 2016, is Election Day.

Will America choose **Marco Rubio?**

Draw YOU as President!

www.ingramcontent.com/pod-product-compliance
Lightning Source LLC
Chambersburg PA
CBHW081542280526
45788CB00010B/3326